NICOLS

Best Walks
around
AVIEMORE

by Richard Hallewell

Illustrations by Rebecca Johnstone

NICOLSON MAPS

3 Frazer St, Largs

Tel. 01475 689242

Published by Nicolson
3 Frazer Street
Largs KA30 9HP

First Published 1998 by Collins
An imprint of HarperCollins*Publishers*
77–85 Fulham Palace Road
London W6 8JB

Copyright © HarperCollins*Publishers* Ltd 1998
Maps © Bartholomew Ltd 1998
www.bartholomewmaps.com

The walks in this guide were first published in
Bartholomew's Walk Loch Ness and the Spey Valley.

Printed in Hong Kong

ISBN 1 86097 094 X
NG10708

CONTENTS

Key map for the walks, key to map symbols   4
Introduction   5

Walk		*Grade*					
Walk 1	Craigellachie	C	WC			🐕	🚌	16
Walk 2	Boat of Garten	C	WC				🚌	17
Walk 3	Sluggan Pass	B	WC	🥾		🐕	🚌	18
Walk 4	Loch Garten	C				🐕		19
Walk 5	Meall a'Bhuachaille	A	WC	🥾			🚌	20
Walk 6	Cairngorm	A	WC	🥾			🚌	22
Walk 7	Serpent's Loch	B	WC			🐕	🚌	24
Walk 8	Loch an Eilein	C	WC			🐕		25
Walk 9	Lower Glen Feshie	B		🥾				26
Walk 10	Upper Glen Feshie	A		🥾				27
Walk 11	Ruthven Barracks	C	WC				🚌	28
Walk 12	Creag Beg	A/B	WC	🥾			🚌	29
Walk 13	Green Bothy	B	WC	🥾			🚌	30
Walk 14	Dun da Lamh	B				🐕		31
Walk 15	Pattack Forest	C				🐕		32

Symbols

WC   Public conveniences available at route, or in nearby town. (NB: these facilities are often closed in winter.)

🥾   Hill walking equipment required. Strong boots; warm waterproof clothing; map and compass for hill routes.

🐕   Route suitable for dogs.

🚌   Public transport available to this route. Details given on individual routes.

Grade

A   Requires a high level of fitness and – for the hill routes – previous experience of hill walking. The use of a detailed map is advised.

B   Requires a reasonable level of fitness. Book map sufficient.

C   A simple, short walk on good paths.

Key map for the walks

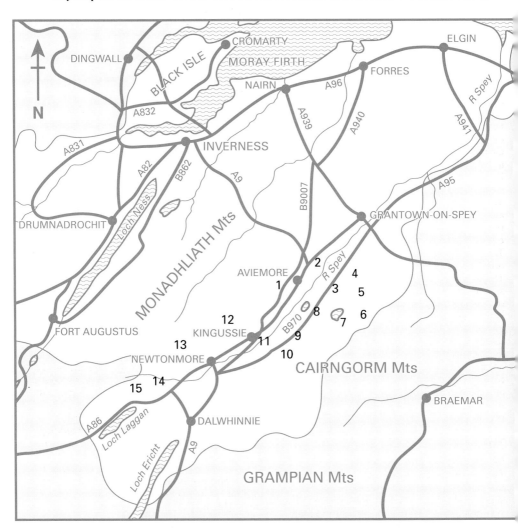

Key to map symbols

● ● ●	Route	⚹⚹ ⚹⚹	Marshland
═══	Metalled Road	...:⁝:...	Moorland
┼┼┼┼┼	Railway	⚘⚘	Coniferous Woodland
Ⓟ	Parking	◈◈	Broad-leaved Woodland
ⓘ	Information Centre	(50m)	Contour : shaded area
⚓	Viewpoint		is above height indicated

4

INTRODUCTION

ABOUT THIS BOOK

This is a book of walks, each of which can be completed within one day. Each route is graded according to its level of difficulty, and wherever specialist hill walking equipment is required this is specified. There is a description of each route, including information on the character and condition of the paths, and with a brief description of the major points of interest along the way. In addition there is a sketch map of the route. Car parks, where available, are indicated on the route maps. The availability of public conveniences and public transport on particular routes is listed on the contents page, and at the head of each route. The suitability or otherwise of the route for dogs is also indicated on the contents page. The location of each route within the area is shown on the key map, and a brief description of how to reach the walk from the nearest town is provided at the start of each walk. National grid references are provided on the maps. The use of a detailed map, in addition to this book, is advised on all grade A walks.

Before setting out, all walkers are asked to read through the section of Advice to Walkers at the end of the Introduction. In the long term it never pays to become lax in taking safety precautions.

THE AREA

(Numbers in italics refer to individual walks.)
The variety of the area's landscape, flora and fauna is a product of its curious, irregular shape, caused by a violent geological history. A mountain is a metaphor for stability, yet it is formed by its own mutability and weakness – the Cairngorms (*6*), for instance, are made of granite – one of the hardest of rocks – yet once they boiled beneath the Earth's crust, finally bursting through the surface and solidifying. They were then carved by the glaciers of the ice age; scraped into the rounded mass they form today. The rocks are not unchanging, they are susceptible to heat and cold and are constantly being altered: sometimes quickly, by volcano and earthquake; sometimes slowly – as today – by rainwater, wind and frost.

The features most easily observed from the routes in this book are those which were formed during the ice age. At its peak, the glaciers covered this entire area, with the exception of a few nunataks – mountain peaks which thrust up above the general level of the ice. The ice moved independently of the area's topographic features, pushed by the great ice sheets of the continent which reached across the North Sea. The ice broke segments of rock from the mountains as it passed; lifted them and, later, as it melted, deposited them. This accounts for the great variety of rock types found on river beds throughout the area – some of them carried from what is now the European mainland – and for the erratics – large rocks, dropped in unlikely positions, on hilltops or in the middle of wide plains.

As the glaciers melted they became smaller and retreated into the higher hills, where the air was cold enough and precipitation high enough to maintain them. Even today, in the cooler north-facing corries of the high hills (*6*), drifts of snow linger well into the summer. If the weather were to become sufficiently cold, over a period of time, these would be the first areas to develop new glaciers.

The glaciers, although reduced in size, continued to move down the valleys; generating ice in the high corries (bowl-shaped depressions in the hillside – common throughout the area) and slowly flowing downhill, until the air temperature was high enough to melt the ice. Several obvious features in the landscape were caused by the ice during this period.

The progress of the glaciers gave the valleys a broad, U-shaped cross-section – very pronounced in glens such as Feshie and Tromie (*9,10,11*) – and left them so enlarged that they are now out of all proportion to the small burns and rivers which meander along their floors. In addition, the valleys of tributary streams, which were less deeply cut by the ice, were left hanging above the level of the main valley floor. The valley floors themselves became filled with the matter scraped from the rocks by the ice – a mixture of fine gravel and small stones – either carried out by the streams of meltwater from the retreating glacier in a deep, even, fluvio-glacial deposit, or left in ridges of hummocky moraine. This gravel is quarried by man, and also by the elements; gradually being eroded by the valley stream and carried down to the river mouth.

The deepest cuts made by the glaciers were along fault lines, where two plates of the Earth's crust meet, and where the rocks are already crushed and weakened. The major fault in the area is along the Great Glen, and it is no coincidence that here the ice excavated Scotland's deepest loch: Loch Ness over 800ft (250m) deep in places. This loch is long and thin; the smaller, rounder lochs are generally kettle holes; pools of water formed where lumps of ice had become embedded in the ground and then, after the main glaciers had retreated, slowly melted. Examples of these lochs are Loch Morlich (7), Loch an Eilein (8) and Loch Garten (4).

HISTORY

The first settlers arrived in the north around 8000 years ago. For thousands of years the few inhabitants lived a nomadic life; wandering through the forests, using only stone tools; as often prey to the hostile environment as predator on its plentiful wildlife. In time, a measure of agriculture became common, and the people began congregating in small settlements and evolving complex burial rituals at set sites – notably, in this area, at Clava, near Inverness.

Around 2500 BC the first few Celts arrived; followed, around 600 BC, by more warlike groups of the same people, with a knowledge of working iron. In later years Celtic came to be associated almost solely with those people living on the periphery of Europe – Brittany, Cornwall, Wales, Ireland and northwest Scotland – but these were only the last strongholds of an extensive race who, at one time, inhabited the bulk of central Europe.

The descriptions of these European Celts, in the work of writers at the time, are illuminating. They portray an open, honest people, with a scorn for subterfuge or ploy, but disposed towards boastfulness and exaggeration; with a great sensitivity to insults, and a tendency to be short-tempered and violent; a lively people with a preference for bright colours, who built no cities, but lived in small villages ruled by local chiefs. This description could have been as easily applied to the Highlanders of the 18th century as to the Celts of the classical authors. Even their mode of battle had not altered; the headlong heedless charge of the clans at Culloden (1746) was precisely that observed by the Roman chroniclers.

One aspect in which the Highlanders did not match their ancestors was in their natural colouring. The European Celts were fair-haired but, despite a later infusion of blood from the similarly blonde Vikings, fair hair is comparatively rare in the modern Highlanders; proof that the earlier residents were not eliminated by the incomers, but integrated.

The Celts continued to arrive – not in concentrated attacks, but in small groups – throughout the next few centuries, bringing with them the various Celtic languages – forerunners of modern Scottish Gaelic, Irish Gaelic, Welsh, Cornish and Manx. They also brought, with their clannishness and warlike disposition, the need for greater defence. They built large forts on easily defended hilltops. Examples of these forts are at Dun da Lamh (14), in a splendid position above the Spey Valley; Farigaig, overlooking Loch Ness; Ord Hill, in the Black Isle; and Creag Phadrig in Inverness. A peculiarity of some of these forts is that their stonework has been fused under intense heat, caused by the ignition of the original wooden framework of the structure. Whether this ignition was accidental, or was intended to strengthen the walls, is a matter of conjecture.

The Romans had arrived in Britain in 78 AD, and had found the islands a patchwork of separate, if broadly related, Celtic tribes. They had quickly subjugated the south, and then moved north, under Agricola, to complete their conquest. Not for the last time, the high hills and narrow passes were to prove a taxing obstacle for an invading army; one, indeed, which the Romans seem to have lacked the energy or inclination, or perhaps the ability, to overcome. The Roman Army marched up the east coast and, somewhere on the eastern fringe of the Grampians, between the River Tay and Inverness, fought a battle against the combined forces of the northern hill tribes. The tribes were led by a man called by the Romans Calgacus – the Swordsman; the earliest recorded name of any Scotsman to have lasted to the present day. His army (of 30,000 men, according to the Roman historian Tacitus) was defeated, and he himself was killed, but the matter is shrouded in the gloom of history.

At any rate, the Roman army immediately withdrew, and made no further, serious, attempts to conquer the Highlands, preferring the expensive and inefficient alternative of building defensive walls across the breadth of the country (Hadrian's Wall in 122 AD; the Antonine Wall in 143 AD), thus allowing the northern tribes free space in which to organise their numerous, and often successful, attacks against their new, unwelcome, neighbours.

The site of Agricola's battle may well be within this area, but no one has been able to identify it with any certainty. The Romans called it Mons Graupius; referring to the northern tribes as Picts, and to the largest tribe of the area as the Caledonians.

Hadrian's Wall was finally overrun in 383 AD, and the Romans departed soon after, leaving the north still free, and as impenetrable to the historian as it had been before they arrived.

The difficulty is partly one of language, for, as different as Welsh is from Gaelic, so was the language of the Picts from either. It was a distinct strain of Celtic, intermingled with the language of the pre-Celtic, bronze age Highlanders, and, although it was in use at least until the 10th century, and probably longer, not a single complete sentence of the language has survived, and nothing which can be translated with certainty.

The Pictish kingdom was a large and a powerful one, covering most of the Highlands and all of the area covered in this book – Inverness was a local capital – yet little remains as proof of the extent of their rule except a few place names and a collection of carved stones. These beautiful monuments are evidence of a distinctive and sophisticated national style, but they are cyphers, as obscure as their makers. They were produced between the 6th and the 9th centuries – a series of slabs, decorated with intermingled images; representational and abstract – and vary in content; pagan, Christian and secular.

For a while the Picts were the ascendant race in Scotland, but, although their descendants are the Scotsmen of today, their culture completely evaporated.

The name Scotland is derived from the Scots – a Celtic tribe who came from Ireland in about 500 AD, and founded a small kingdom in Argyll, called Dalriada.

With the arrival of the Scots a pale beam of light once more illuminates Scottish history. These immigrants brought with them Gaelic, Christianity and writing, and with the last they kept the first scant records of Scottish life.

The most famous of the Scots was Columba. He was born a nobleman, but became a churchman; combining his role as a religious leader with that of a politician. In 565 AD he journeyed up the Great Glen to meet with Brude, King of the Picts, at Inverness. This trip is best remembered as the occasion of the first recorded mention of a large, unusual creature in Loch Ness, but it was successful in more ways than that. Columba had two main objectives in his embassage; firstly, to gain permission to send his acolytes throughout Pictland to establish religious foundations; and, secondly, to sue for peace for the Scots – who had been overrun by the more powerful Picts since their arrival on the west coast – to allow them to expand their territories. In the long run, the granting of the former request virtually conceded the latter. From that moment the Gaelic, Latin and Christian culture of the Scots began to replace that of the Picts. The political unification of the two nations followed in 843 AD, and seems to have been a relatively bloodless business, by the extravagantly sanguine standards of the time.

The move towards unity was accelerated by the attacks of the Vikings – who had begun to trouble both nations from around 800 AD – and was sealed by a peculiarity of Pictish law: the descent of power was matrilineal. In effect, this meant that the successor to a king would not be his son, but his sister's son, or his daughter's son; thus, when the Pictish King's daughter married the Scottish King, Alpin, the resulting son, Kenneth, was heir to the crowns of both kingdoms, which he duly inherited.

The Vikings colonised the north of Scotland and the islands, but in this area they never moved south of the Black Isle in any numbers. Certainly, their paganism made little impression on the Christian Church of the area, which had flourished since the time of Columba.

By the time King Malcolm II died, in 1034, Scotland – although it lacked the islands to the north and west; still in the hands of the Norsemen – was, in extent, largely as it is today. Malcolm was a Gaelic-speaking king of a Gaelic people; with the exception of the remaining Vikings and Picts in the north, a few Welsh-speaking Britons in Strathclyde, and the Germanic people of Lothian. Prior to his death, however, he broke with the Celtic tradition of tanistry – whereby the crown was passed between various branches of the royal family;

thereby ensuring a sovereign of suitable age and ability – and gave the crown to his daughter's son, Duncan. Not unnaturally, there was considerable displeasure among the nobles who considered themselves the rightful claimants: principally, Thorfinn the Mighty, Earl of Orkney, and MacBeth, Mormaer of Ross and Moray (Mormaer was an old Pictish term for a powerful regional ruler). MacBeth – who had a castle at Inverness – defeated Duncan, somewhere in Moray or the Black Isle, and killed him. He ruled Scotland (or, as the Gaelic-speakers called it, Alba) for seventeen years, and was generally considered a good king, before he himself was killed by Duncan's son, Malcolm Ceann Mor (Great leader) – a man brought up in England, who introduced many Anglo-Saxon followers, with their feudal culture and laws, in the wake of his victory.

The importance of this episode was that it marked the end of the Celtic royalty of Alba, and the start of the Anglo-Norman kingship of Scotland. The capital was moved from Dunfermline to Edinburgh – that is, from Celtic Fife to Norman Lothian. The Scottish kings now represented a minority in the kingdom, and, as a result, did not have the power to intimidate either the Celtic Highlanders, who continued to live much as they always had, or the Scottish nobles, who, by creating an alliance with anyone – French, English or Highland – could create havoc in this small, politically unbalanced country. Thus, the seeds of the problems which were to beset Scotland for the next seven centuries were set: a nobility and royalty forced into continual intrigue with foreign powers; and a people so divided by culture and language that, even in the nation's darkest moments, they could never be compelled to work together.

In the centuries following Duncan's accession the politics of the area degenerated into local power struggles. The War of Independence, which climaxed with Bruce's victory over Edward II of England at Bannockburn, in 1314, was treated by most of the Celtic families as an opportunity to gamble for gain. When Bruce began his campaign his chances of victory seemed slight, so those with the most to lose opposed him (notably, in this area, the Comyns; a family of great power, who had the added incentive that Bruce had murdered John Comyn – a rival claimant to the throne – at the start of his campaign), while those with more to gain took the gamble on Bruce, and reaped their rewards in the wake of

his unexpected success. Most of the clans prominent in this area in later years came out for Bruce at Bannockburn: Fraser, Grant, Mackintosh, MacPherson and Gordon. It is worth noting that, at this time, it was still common for families to move from one side of the Highland line to the other – Fraser and Grant were both French names originally, and Gordon is a place name in the Borders; but, as time went on, the Highlands became more insular, and such movement less common.

In 1371 Bruce's line failed, and the Stewarts came to power. The early Stewarts lived in bad times, but they were not especially bad kings. They had, in varying measures, considerable wit and energy, but it was largely dissipated resolving disputes with their southern magnates. They all came to the throne young, and spent most of their reigns clearing up the mess created by a succession of regents during their minorities; before invariably dying, just as it seemed that order might be restored, and leaving the nation, once again, to the incompetent or dishonest regents. The policies which they followed in the Highlands were frequently heavy-handed, but the Stewarts had considerable Highland blood, and they seemed genuinely involved in the affairs of the north. All the Stewarts, up to Mary, Queen of Scots, spoke Gaelic fluently, and remained proud of their Celtic ancestry. Their policies – generally leaving Highland affairs in the hands of one or two powerful families, who could then be played against each other to keep them from uniting against the crown – were often unpopular with their Highland subjects, but, in later years, the Highlanders remembered the Stewarts with some affection, as the last royal house in which they could sense a measure of understanding, if not of sympathy.

It may seem strange that the Highlanders, given the purity and distinction of their culture within a strictly defined area – above the Highland Line – never formed a state of their own; particularly since there was more than enough martial power within the area to defend it against the weak Scottish crown. The nearest that the Highlanders came to such a state was under the MacDonald Lords of the Isles who, for a while, held unrestricted powers in the north and west. In 1462 a treaty was signed between John MacDonald, Lord of the Isles – styling himself as an independent ruler; the Earl of Douglas – representing the most powerful family of the southern nobility; and

King Edward IV of England; agreeing to ally themselves to remove the Stewarts, and then to divide Scotland between them.

The plan was never put into operation, but the treaty was discovered, and the power of the Lordship of the Isles waned from then on. Its court had been the centre of Gaelic culture and learning, and the only tenable power base entirely sustained from within the Highland area; so, when the Lordship of the Isles reverted to the crown in 1493 it was not simply the learning, the libraries and the records which were lost, it was also the only plausible chance of internal rule. It was never a likely occurrence in any case; the Highland society was the antithesis of the modern state: a society rooted in anarchism, not as an obscure ideal, but as a living fact. As the power of the MacDonalds grew it cast the shadow of authority over their Highland neighbours, who did not care for authority of any sort, and were among the quickest to profit when fortune turned against the MacDonalds. A great deal of idealism has been attributed to the Highlanders, but their love of personal freedom was a practical one. No clan enjoyed having powerful neighbours.

One man who wielded considerable power in this area during the early years of the Stewart dynasty was Alexander Stewart – the Wolf of Badenoch – a son of Robert II, and the king's representative in the Highlands. His main fortresses were at Lochindorb (north of Grantown-on-Spey), Ruthven (on the site of the present remains) (*11*) and Loch an Eilein (*8*). In 1390 he burnt the town and cathedral of Elgin in response to a slight from the bishop. It is worth noting that such behaviour was considered irrational and violent even at the time.

It was during this period that the clan system reached its zenith. The system was not unique to the Highlands – it was the direct descendant of the tribal divisions of the Celtic race, common, at one time, throughout central Europe – but, due to the remoteness of the Highlands, the language differences, and the lack of the will, or the strength, on the part of the Scottish monarchy, to force significant change upon the people, this archaic system lasted, in this area, into relatively modern times; the period of Empire and enlightenment.

Clann means children, but clan membership was always more flexible than that, with various families, individuals and other clans willing to give allegiance to a local chief for the safety of living within a group. The clansmen were genuinely loyal to their chiefs, but expected loyalty in return. It was not unknown for a leader to be deposed by his own people, if they felt he had proved himself unworthy.

It was a warrior society, where a chief's wealth was reckoned in men at arms; where bravery was a primary virtue, and had to be proved. In such a society life was not valued as highly as it is in our own, while honour was everything. A relatively minor insult could be the cause of a bloody and protracted feud; often lasting for generations.

This dangerous world seemed to give the people a heightened sensitivity to poetry and music, which the life of the 17th-century cateran James MacPherson typifies. MacPherson was a thug – a cattle riever and terrorist – and yet he was also a respected composer and fiddle player. Some of his compositions are still played today; including MacPherson's Rant and MacPherson's Lament; the two pieces he played by his gallows before he was hanged (his final act was to break his fiddle across his knee; the instrument is now in the Clan MacPherson museum in Newtonmore).

A chief might reckon his wealth in men, but his finances depended on cattle. Cattle raids were a central part of Highland culture, and so were the summer and autumn cattle drives. Each year great herds of fattened beasts were driven through the hills to the lowland markets. Some of the routes in this book follow the rough tracks they used, through narrow glens and across hill passes (*9,10*).

The women and children of the clans lived a life of transhumance: spending their winters with the menfolk and the animals, all living together in small, dark, heather-thatched cottages in the lower glens; and, in the spring, moving with the cattle to the shielings – small huts in the high pastures. The remains of the shielings can often be seen in the higher glens. (There is a museum of Highland housing and agricultural practices in Kingussie.)

In 1603, James VI became King of both Scotland and England. In the wars which coloured the reigns of the last of the Stewarts (James, Charles I, Charles II and James VI and II), the north saw much of the action. Graham of Montrose, the finest general ever to lead a Highland army, won a sequence of dazzling victories for the Catholic Charles I against the presbyterian Covenanters (including the Battle of Auldearn, near Nairn, in 1645); and Graham of Claverhouse – Bonnie Dundee – was victorious for James VII at Killiecrankie. These were wars of religious ideology, but, however committed their generals were to the cause, the clans were committed only to profit and revenge. They watched to see which side their enemies joined, and joined the other.

In 1707 the Treaty of Union joined the parliaments of Scotland and England. In an independent Scotland the Highlands had been an area of considerable, ungovernable power; in the context of Great Britain it was simply a troublesome province.

By 1715 the clans were in rebellion, partly for the restoration of a Catholic, Stewart monarch (William and Mary had taken the throne of James VII in 1689) and partly in protest against the Union. The 1715 rebellion was a shambles, and, following its disintegration, General Wade was sent north from England to supervise the pacification of the Highlands. This he did, partly by raising regiments from the local population – more suited to the warfare of the terrain than were his own troops – and partly by building the first planned roads in the Highlands. These roads connected a series of forts, including Ruthven Barracks (*11*), Fort William, Fort Augustus and Fort George, at Inverness. All of these have now disappeared with the exception of the ruins of Ruthven. Fort George was rebuilt along the coast, in 1769: it is a vast complex; still in use, but open to the public.

General Wade's Road is a common phrase on Highland maps: either alongside later, motor-roads, which have followed his original routes, or by the steep, hill tracks, now used only by hill walkers. The A9 follows one of his routes, as does the A86 from Newtonmore to Spean Bridge (*15*).

The Highlanders were not at all happy to have their glens made more accessible – their strongest defence had always been inaccessibility – but the roads proved a great boon to later travellers. In the words of the famous couplet:

Had you seen these roads before they were made,/ You would lift up your hands and bless General Wade.

There was a second Jacobite rising in 1745. The Stewart cause depended on the support of the Catholic clans, and of those others who wished to strike at the hand of Hanoverian authority. The most powerful clans of the time, in this area, were the MacPhersons, in upper Strathspey; the Grants, in lower Strathspey; the

Mackintoshes of Strath Dearn and Strath Nairn; the Frasers of Loch Ness and the Aird; the Chisholms of Glen Affric; and the Mackenzies, who held land in the Black Isle. The farmland of Nairn and Moray was owned by a number of smaller estates. It is difficult to make snap statements about who supported the Jacobite cause and who did not – many of the clans were divided – however, the Grants were broadly Hanoverian, and the balance broadly Jacobite. The Mackintoshes serve as an example of the divisions. The clan chief held a commission in the Black Watch – one of the government's Highland regiments – and remained Hanoverian throughout. His wife, on the other hand – Colonel Anne – was a Jacobite, and raised a force from the clan for the Stewarts.

In all, only 6000 Highlanders joined the Stewart cause – evidence of a general scepticism – but all the clans, Jacobite and Hanoverian alike, were punished in the aftermath of a battle which ended not only the rebellion, but also the power of the clans – Culloden. The battle site is a few miles to the east of Inverness, and is maintained by the National Trust for Scotland. It is a forlorn spot; a monument to a battle where nothing was won, and a whole way of life was lost.

Prince Charles Edward Stewart fled the battlefield and, after many adventures, the country. The selfless courage shown by many Highlanders, both supporters and opponents, in effecting his escape was quite remarkable. Similarly touching is the loyalty shown by the people of the clan MacPherson. Their chief, a leading Jacobite, was hunted by the government troops. He hid for nine years in a cave (on Creag Dubh, near Newtonmore) without being given away, despite the offer of a vast reward for his capture.

The hardships endured by the Highlanders at the hands of the victorious Hanoverian army, led by the Duke of Cumberland, were compounded by the insults of the ensuing legislation. Not only was the Disarming Act – first introduced after the 1715 rebellion – reinforced, but the people were banned from wearing the Highland tartans, under the threat of deportation. In addition, no effort was spared to impress upon the people the inferiority of their language and lifestyle.

Following Culloden, many of the clan chiefs, needing to establish themselves under the new regime, raised regiments from their clansmen, to fight for the Hanoverians. These regiments acquitted themselves with great bravery, and disproportionate loss, in Europe and America, for a country which was only too glad to see the back of them.

This was also the sentiment of an increasing number of clan chiefs, who were now, deprived of their ancient powers and responsibilities, little more than landlords of vast, unprofitable estates. Their need was more for money than for men.

All the Highland towns are products of this period: clearance towns, built to take the overspill when the glens were cleared of men and cattle to make way for sheep – more profitable tenants of the land.

Many Highlanders, unwilling to accept the new conditions, and often financially encouraged by their chiefs, emigrated; usually to a better life. Others, not wishing to leave the country, moved to the new harbours along the coast and took to the herring fishery; a hard and dangerous life, chasing the *silver darlings* in an open boat. Others took jobs building the roads and railways or – at the start of the 19th century – Telford's Caledonian Canal.

The suppression of the spirit of the remaining Highlanders was so swift and successful that, within a hundred years of Culloden, the Highlands were safe enough to have became fashionable.

The transformation was largely triggered by a gradual appreciation of the bravery and effectiveness of the Highland regiments, and also by the work of James Ossian MacPherson – the successful perpetrator of one of the finest literary frauds of all time. MacPherson was born at Ruthven (11) in 1736, and worked, for a while, as a tutor. In 1760 he published his first translations of ancient Gaelic epics, originally written by the 3rd-century bard, Ossian. Folk tales of Ossian and the Fingalian warriors were common enough in Scotland and Ireland, but MacPherson's epics, in their turgid, hollow English, were all his own work. His tales of misty heroism were extraordinarily popular. His work was compared to Homer's; it swept across Europe, influencing Goethe, inspiring Napoleon, and signalling the start of the Romantic movement. In addition, it brought its author a seat in parliament, a large estate on Speyside and a burial at Westminster Abbey. There is a monument to this most successful and least read of Scottish authors at Balavil, near Kingussie.

The romanticising of the Highlands was completed by Queen Victoria and Prince Albert, who purchased Balmoral Castle, in Deeside, in 1852. They made tartan and pipe-bands fashionable, and started a vogue for Highland holidays which led directly to the development of the north-south rail links and the growth of the towns along the lines. At the same time the estates, which were now owned by men who made their fortunes outside the Highlands, and who could afford to maintain the lands for leisure, were turned into sporting estates, with deer stalking, grouse shooting and salmon fishing.

These estates are still in operation today, as are the fishing ports and the sheep farms. More recently developed forms of employment include commercial forestry – which is rife throughout the area – hydro-electric power and the expansion of the tourist industry – including the development of the winter sports facilities in the Cairngorms.

One other old industry has lasted the years. The place names of lower Speyside should be music to the ear of any great whisky drinker, for this area has the greatest concentration of malt distilleries in the country.

PLACE NAMES

The original meanings of place names are often obscured by time and language. This problem is particularly acute in the north where place names are derived from at least five separate cultures: pre-Celtic, Pictish, Scandinavian, Gaelic and English. The names of the larger rivers – Spey, Findhorn, Ness, etc – would seem to be the most antiquated, being derived from roots common throughout Europe, and predating the Celtic peoples. They are totally obscure.

Surviving Pictish names are rare, but the geographical range of this people throughout Scotland, when they existed as a separate race, can be accurately traced by one particular prefix – pit – which is a Pictish word signifying a piece of land and seems to have been adopted by the later Gaelic people to distinguish originally Pictish settlements – eg, Pitmain (near Kingussie), Pittendreich (near Elgin) and others.

Scandinavian place names, brought by the Vikings, are rare in this area, but there are some, generally distorted or blended with Gaelic elements, in the Black Isle – eg, Udale and Culbo.

The Scots names (ie, the Scots or Lallans dialect of English) are commonest on the coastal plain of Moray, and the further east one looks the commoner they become. This is because the people of the eastern areas changed from speaking Gaelic to speaking Scots at an earlier period than did those of the western areas. Later still, English-speaking landowners began providing names. Moray contains the full range – eg, Carn na Cailliche (Gaelic), Hempriggs and Paddockhaugh (Scots) and Newton and Charlestown (English).

By far the greatest number of names in this area are of Gaelic origin. A list of the commonest elements in Gaelic place names is given below, but don't be surprised if the map spelling differs from that shown below: this is partly due to the anglicisation of the words and partly to Gaelic grammar, which causes nouns and adjectives to alter, depending on their use in the sentence. One final tip – in the Gaelic the adjective generally follows the noun: eg, Cairngorm – Blue Hill, Monadhliath – Grey Moor. Translations are given of place names in the text, where they are of particular interest.

Common elements in place names (Gaelic unless otherwise stated):
aber – confluence
abhainn – river
acarsaid – harbour
ach/Achadh – field
allt – burn
aird – promontory
-ay/-ey – island (Norse)
bal/baile – town, settlement
beag/beg – small
bealach – hill pass
beinn/ben – mountain
breac – speckled
buidhe – yellow
camas – bay
carn/cairn – hill, heap of stones
cnoc/knock – hillock
coire – corrie (hollow)
creag/craig – rock, cliff
dale/dal – valley (Norse)
dubh – black
dun – steep hill, fort
eilean – island
firth – arm of the sea (Norse)
glas – Grey
inver – river mouth
kil – church
kyle/caol – narrow strait

leacann – slope
leitir – extensive slope
lochan – small loch
meall – rounded hill
mor – big
ruadh – red
rubha – point of land
sgeir/skerry – rock surrounded by sea
sgurr – peak, sharp top
sron – nose, point
stac – rocky column, cliff
storr – steep, high peak
tobar – well
-val – mountain (Norse)

NATURAL HISTORY

The area can usefully be divided into a number of distinct environments, which recur along the various routes in this book – **native caledonian pine forest, commercial forestry, native broad-leaved woodland, mountain and moorland, freshwater.**

Caledonian pine forest (4,5,8). The **Scots pine** is the only obvious conifer indigenous to the British Isles, and forests containing this species, along with native broad-leaved woodland including **birch, oak, rowan, alder, willow** and **ash**, once covered much of the Scottish Highlands. Nowadays the natural forest exists only in a few small, protected pockets. In this area the main native remnants are around the Cairngorms in the south, and in Glen Affric in the west.

The **Scots pine** is distinguished by its pale pink/brown bar, and by the dark, bottle green of its needles. In its early years it grows straight and conical, but later, given the space to spread out, it can develop into a number of shapes.

A typical Caledonian pine forest consists almost entirely of the one species of tree, interspersed with **birch, rowan** and **alder**.

Beneath the trees is a thick mat of **bell** and **ling heather, blaeberry, cowberry** and various mosses. In the Speyside forests there is also considerable **juniper** – a dark springy shrub which can grow in low thickets, or as a single plant, up to 25ft (7.5m) in height.

The forest contains a wide array of the smaller birds: **blue, great coal tits, treecreeper, bullfinch, chaffinch** and **wren**, as well as the more particular **goldcrest** and **siskin**, and the localised conifer specialists: **crested tit** and **Scottish crossbill** (4,5,8).

Of the larger birds, the most spectacular is the **capercaillie** – the largest of the native grouse. The cock is large, black and not unlike a turkey; but it is more likely to be heard, crashing through the branches of trees, than seen.

There is not a great deal of animal life peculiar to the forest, but **roe** and **red deer** are likely to be seen – the latter especially during the colder months, when they come down from the hills in search of grazing. **Red squirrels** are common in this area. Of the carnivores, **fox**, **badger**, **stoat**, **wildcat**, **otter** and **weasel** all inhabit the forest. The **pine marten**, once nearly extinct but now expanding in numbers and range, lives in both native and commercial forests.

Commercial forestry *(3,5,7,9,10,14,15)* In their early stages, the woodlands formed through re-afforestation lack the diversity of the native Caledonian forest. Nevertheless, they are important wildlife habitat and are currently managed in a multi-objective way including maximising opportunities for wildlife conservation. This process becomes more prominent as the woods mature, and are harvested and replanted using carefully considered design plans. The bird and animal life is largely that of the Caledonian forest, but may be harder to see in dense woodland.

Of major interest is the variety of conifer types which are now planted. The list includes **Scots pine**; **Sitka** and **Norway spruce**; **Japanese**, **European** and **hybrid larch**; **Douglas fir**; **western red hemlock** and a great many others. Most of the routes listed above pass through entirely commercial plantations, but in some the conifers are older, and widely spaced.

Broad-leaved woodland *(1)*. Although only one of the routes is listed as passing through predominantly broad-leaved woodland, most of them pass through some. The commonest species of broad-leaved trees in this area are **birch**, **rowan**, **alder** and **oak**, although **beech**, **ash**, **hawthorn**, **holly** and others also appear. In the Highlands **birch**, which grows up to 2000ft (600m), is by far the commonest broad-leaved tree. Craigellachie Wood *(1)* is entirely of **birch**, and is maintained as a nature reserve.

A great variety of grasses, flowers, mosses, and lichens grow in these woods, while large areas – particularly in the birch woods – are covered in **bracken**.

Most of the larger mammals exist in woodland throughout the area, the **rabbit, fox, badger, hedgehog, weasel, stoat** and **roe deer** of the lower woods being supplemented by the **wildcat** and **red deer** (in the colder months) in the higher wooded glens.

A wide variety of tits, warblers, pipits and finches inhabit the woods; the **long-tailed tit** being particularly drawn to the birch woods. In addition, **woodcock, mistle** and **song thrush**, **blackbird** and **wren** are likely to be seen. **Buzzard** and **kestrel** also nest in these woods.

Mountains and moorland *(5,6,10,11,12,13)* The Highlands are famous for their moors: vast areas of heather which give a purple shade to the hillsides from July to September. They seem empty, yet these moors are of considerable interest to naturalists, and are a central part of the local economy – as are sheep runs, grouse moors and deer forests – so be careful not to disturb the wildlife, and always check with estates, tourist information centres and local people before walking on the moors from August onwards, when grouse shooting and deer stalking may be in progress.

The plant life which constitutes the moors varies greatly, depending on which direction the moor slopes, its height above sea level, and the underlying rock or soil. Flat areas of moorland are often floating on a considerable depth of peat: a mass of black, sodden, half-rotted vegetation, which provides effective fuel when dried. These peat moors *(13)* tend to be very wet, and pools and bogs of dark water often develop. These encourage plants such as **bog cotton, bog asphodel** and the pungent **bog myrtle**. For the most part, however, the moors are predominantly of **ling heather**, with **bell heather, blaeberry** and other shrubs intermixed. On the mountain slopes the **ling** gives way to a covering of **blaeberry, crowberry, dwarf juniper** and others.

Parts of the moor are burnt in the spring, to encourage new growth in the heather to feed the **red grouse**. **Grouse** are common up to 3000ft (900m), and are frequently seen springing up from the heather and flying off swiftly, giving a strange, nasal call, generally transcribed as *go back, go back, go back*. Other birds to be seen on the lower moors include the **skylark, stonechat, wheatear** and **curlew**. **Crows** are present here, as everywhere: both the **carrion** and grey cowled **hooded crow**.

The **red deer** are high in the hills during the summer – partly to escape the fierce insect life of the summer moors – but return to the lower moors in the autumn, and can often be seen from the main roads during the winter. **Wildcat, fox** and **stoat** are present, although generally unseen, along with the **blue hare** – slightly smaller than the common variety – which, like the stoat, turns white during the winter months.

Another creature which camouflages itself against the winter snow fields by turning white is the **ptarmigan** (6). This bird – the hardiest of the grouse family – will only venture below 2500ft (750m) in the severest winter weather, otherwise remaining on the sub-arctic hilltops. These hilltops – particularly in the Cairngorms – are an example of how much of Scotland must have looked some 10,000 years ago, just after the last ice age. No plant can grow to any size, because of the extremely short growing season and the high winds, so the cover is of dwarf shrubs, sheltering between the broken rocks of the summits. Apart from the **ptarmigan**, few birds exist at this height, but the Cairngorms (6) have a few dotterel and snow bunting near the peaks.

One creature which existed in Scotland until the 9th century – the **reindeer** – has been re-introduced, and grazes on the lichens in the Cairngorms. These are quite tame and harmless.

The commonest of the birds of prey throughout the area is the **buzzard**, but there is always a chance of seeing a **kestrel, peregrine** or **merlin** on the moors; or even, in the more remote glens, a **golden eagle**.

Flowers in the ditches, hedgerow, pastureland and woodland are abundant and varied.

Freshwater (2,4,7,8,9,10,12) This is rather a broad grouping, incorporating low level lochs, hill burns and moorland peat bogs. A great deal of water falls on the Highlands, eventually reaching the sea via a teeming network of bogs, burns, ponds, falls, lochans, lochs and rivers, so most of the routes in this book pass likely habitats along the way – only those routes where the water is a central feature are listed above.

The **bog cotton, asphodel** and **myrtle** and various mosses of the peat bogs give way to largely woodland plants as the small burns pass through their high-sided, narrow glens. Various pondweeds, reeds, sedges and grasses are common by the lochs and lochans, along with **water lily, water lobelia** and others.

The most famous of Scottish water birds – the **osprey** – nests in this area. This splendid bird is no longer as rare as it once was, and can be seen fishing at many of the lochs throughout the area. There is a hide at the nesting site on Loch Garten (4).

Duck are very common at all stages of the rivers' development, with **mallard** and **teal** as high as the moor's edge, and **wigeon, pochard, goldeneye, red-breasted merganser, tufted duck** and **goosander** in the lower waters.

Also by the upper waters are **redshank, curlew** and **lapwing**; while **dippers** and **grey** and **pied wagtails** are common in the shaded dens.

None of the routes in this book passes close to the nesting areas of the **red-throated** or **black-throated diver** – the high lochans, specifically chosen for their isolation – but both species nest within this area, and may be seen flying overhead.

The variety of freshwater fish in the area is not great, but those species which do exist do so in great numbers. The most common of all is the **brown trout** – resident in most bodies of water – and the most important is the **Atlantic salmon**, which ascends the rivers during the summer, to spawn in the headwaters at the end of the year. These fish can be seen jumping in rivers throughout the area, the Spey and Findhorn being particularly noted salmon rivers. In the lochs there are **pike** and **perch** in great numbers, **eels** and, in the deeper lochs, **char** – a distant cousin of the salmon.

There are few mammals which specifically live by the water, but one – the **otter** – is not uncommon throughout the area, although it is quite rare to see one. Other swimmers include **water vole** and **mink**.

Many of these species are shy and sensitive to intrusion, so it is important to disturb them as little as possible. The walker is in no danger from the wildlife of the area, although, as a general rule, it is wise to stay clear of any creature with young. Of the domestic animals, **sheepdogs** can be a nuisance, but are generally bluffing; **bulls**, on the other hand, should never be approached, however lethargic they may appear.

There is one poisonous snake in the area – the **adder**. It is rare to see one – usually coiled in a patch of sunlight, somewhere quiet – and even rarer to be bitten. **Adders** are extremely shy and will always move if they sense anyone approaching. Anyone who is bitten should consult a doctor. Bites are not lethal, but they give rise to an unpleasant, temporary illness.

Two insects are deserving of note. The **cleg**, or **horse fly**, is very common, particularly in moorland areas, and delivers an irritating bite. Even more numerous, and the bane of the outdoor enthusiast's life, is the **midge**. These diminutive insects tend to congregate around water, but, since water is virtually omnipresent in this area, they are rather difficult to avoid. There are a number of creams and sprays to deter them, but they generally find a way through the best prepared defences. Midges are particularly active around sunset.

ADVICE TO WALKERS

Always check the weather forecast before setting off on the longer walks and prepare yourself for the walk accordingly. Remember that an excess of sunshine – causing sunburn or dehydration – can be just as debilitating as snow or rain, and carry adequate cover for your body in all conditions when on the hills.

Snow cover on higher slopes often remains well into the summer and should be avoided by inexperienced walkers as it often covers hidden watercourses and other pitfalls which are likely to cause injury. Also soft snow is extremely gruelling to cross and can sap energy quickly. Walking on snow-covered hills should not be attempted without an ice axe and crampons.

The other weather-associated danger on the hills is the mist, which can appear very swiftly and cut visibility to a few yards. A map and compass should always be carried while on the higher hills.

Obviously these problems are unlikely to arise on the shorter, simpler routes, but it is always wise when out walking to anticipate the worst and to be ready for it. The extra equipment may never be needed, but it is worth taking anyway, just in case. Spare food, a first aid kit, a whistle and a torch with a spare battery should be carried on all hill walks. In addition, details of your route and expected time of return should be left with someone, who you should advise on your safe return.

From August onwards there is grouse shooting and deer stalking on the moors. If you are undertaking one of the hill routes, first check with the local estate or tourist office, thereby avoiding a nuisance for the sportsmen and possible danger to yourself.

COUNTRY CODE

All walkers, when leaving public roads to pass through farmland, forestry or moorland, should respect the interests of those whose livelihood depends on the land. Carelessness can easily cause damage. You are therefore urged to follow the Country Code:

Guard against all risk of fire.

Keep all dogs under proper control (especially during the lambing season – April and May).

Fasten all gates.

Keep to the paths across farmland.

Avoid damaging fences, hedges and walls.

Leave no litter.

Safeguard water supplies.

Protect wildlife, wild plants and trees.

Go carefully on country roads.

Respect the life of the countryside.

1 Craigellachie

Length: 2 miles (3km)
Height climbed: 250ft (80m)
Grade: C
Public conveniences: Aviemore
Public transport: Bus and train services to
Aviemore from north and south

A short walk through natural birch wood,
with its distinctive wildlife. Paths good,
but slippery when wet.

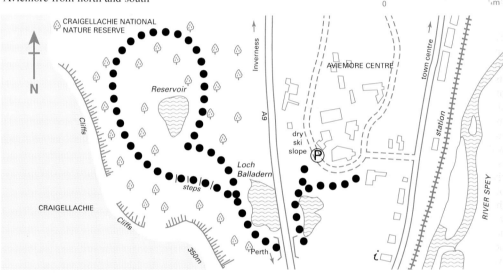

Directly behind Aviemore is Craigellachie *(The Watch Hill)*. The name of the hill was the caithgairm, or war cry, of the clan Grant. The lower slopes of this hill are clothed in mature, natural birch woodland; the upper is steep and rocky - the nesting place of jackdaws and often, peregrine falcons. A section of the hill is now a National Nature Reserve.

Park in the large car park by the dry ski slope opposite the Badenoch Hotel. Skirt the exercise area behind the lochan, and cut right, through the tunnel under the A9. The path is clearly marked from there on.

The way is steep in places and there are quite a number of steps along the way, while a good part of the route is on raised wooden slats — these can become very slippery if it has been raining.

Follow signs for the longer trail, and the arrows on cairns along the route.

The animal life in the birch wood consists largely of the smaller mammals — mice and voles. Bird life, apart from the peregrines, includes a great many of the smaller species: tits and finches, goldcrest, wren, wagtail and siskin. A complete list is provided in a leaflet available in Aviemore.

From the higher section of the walk there is a fine view across Aviemore and Speyside to the Cairngorms. The ski slopes beyond Loch Morlich are visible on clear days.

Because of the nesting falcons visitors are asked to stay on the paths, particularly if walking between April and July — the nesting period.

2 Boat of Garten

Length: 2 miles (3km)
Height climbed: None
Grade: C
Public conveniences: Boat of Garten
Public transport: Bus service between Aviemore and Grantown-on-Spey

A short walk along the banks of the River Spey, through fields and mixed woodland. The path is likely to be wet in places and there are a number of stiles to be crossed.

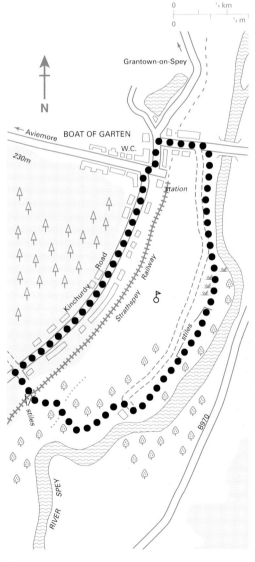

The Spey is the second longest river in Scotland, and Boat of Garten is about midway along its course: approximately 40 miles (65km) south of its mouth at Spey Bay and 45 miles (70km) north of its source at Loch Spey. This route follows a short stretch of the river. Boat of Garten is 5 miles (8km) north of Aviemore, just off the A95 road to Grantown-on-Spey. Park in the town and walk down to the bridge over the river. The town is named after the ferry which used to cross the river at this point. The ferryboat cottage is now a private house. Just before the bridge turn right through a gate by a bench. The path follows the very edge of the river and can be very damp. In addition there are a number of stiles to be negotiated along the way, but it is a pleasant walk, initially through mixed broad-leaved woodland and then through fields. Watch out for water fowl on the river. When the path reaches the white house at Wester Dalvoult turn right, just before the house, and follow the path to a junction at the foot of a steep slope. Turn left here. The path skirts around the hill and where the track curves left, turn right on a clear path into a pleasant area of mixed woodland. Carry straight on, crossing the railway line. This is the Strathspey Railway: a steam line running between Aviemore and Boat of Garten. There are plans to extend this line to Grantown-on-Spey. Beyond the railway the path cuts through a wood of Scots pine before joining Kinchurdy Road. Turn right here, along a metalled road, to return to the old town.

3 Sluggan Pass

Length: 6 miles (9.5km) there and back
Height climbed: 450ft (130m)
Grade: B
Public conveniences: Glenmore
Public transport: Bus service between Aviemore and the ski slopes; stops at Glenmore

A forest walk on good roads leading to a steep-sided pass, with possible extensions.

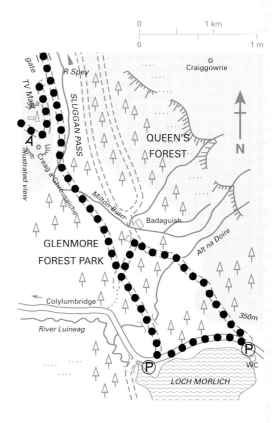

The Kincardine Hills are an arm of the Cairngorm Mountains, severed from the main body of the hills by the Ryvoan Pass *(27)*. The Sluggan *(Gullet)* is a narrow hill between the two most westerly peaks of the range: Creag a'Chreusaiche *(Shoemaker's Hill)* and Craiggowrie *(Goat Hill)*.

To reach this walk turn off the B970 at Coylumbridge and follow the road to Loch Morlich. The route starts at the west end of the loch.

Start walking up the path signposted to Milton of Kincardine. The early part of the way is through Scots pine forest — most of it recently planted but interspersed with relics of the original forest, some of them very large. From the end of the path, at the boundary of the Queen's Forest, there are two possible extensions. One leads to the peak of Creag a'Ghreusaiche, the other descends by the Milton Burn to the Spey Valley — a further 1½ miles (2.5km). The view from the creag is splendid (see below), if rather obscured by trees. Do not interfere with the television aerial or building at the summit.

An alternative return route is shown on the map, leading past Badaguish to Glenmore.

1. *Creag Dhubh (848m)* **2.** *The Cairngorms and Loch Morlich* **3.** *Ord Ban (428m)* **4.** *Coylumbridge* **5.** *Loch Alvie* **6.** *Monadhliath Mountains* **7.** *Craigellachie* **8.** *Aviemore*

4 Loch Garten

Length: 2 miles (3km)
Height climbed: None
Grade: C
Public conveniences: None
Public transport: None

A short, pleasant track through the Scots pine woodland of the RSPB nature reserve, famous for its Ospreys. Path good.

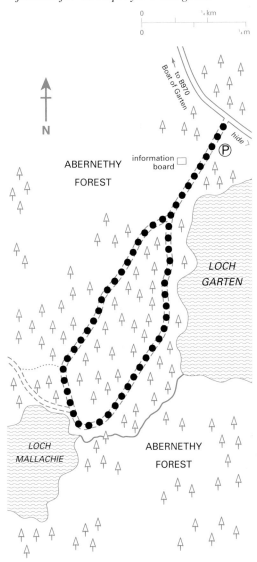

Loch Garten is known to most people through its association with ospreys. These birds had not been seen in Scotland since the early part of the 20th century until a pair nested at Loch Garten in 1959, and their numbers throughout the Highlands have been increasing ever since. There is a hide above Loch Garten from which the nesting birds can be viewed. To reach the walk, turn into Boat of Garten off the A95 between Aviemore and Grantown-on-Spey. Cross the bridge over the River Spey and turn left at the junction on to the B970. Take the first turn to the right. The car park is 1 mile (1.5km) along this road, on the right. The path is very clear: forking soon after it reaches Loch Garten. There are many small tracks down to the lochside but it makes no difference which fork is taken as the path runs in a loop, up to the edge of Loch Mallachie. The wood is semi-natural Scots pine — many of the trees are very old, while others have been planted recently. This type of woodland encourages the specialist bird life — in particular the crested tit, Scottish crossbill and capercaillie, which — in this country — only breed in the conifer forests of the Highlands. Watch also for water fowl on the lochs. An information board at the start of the walk marks longer trails.

5 Meall a'Bhuachaille

Length: 6½ miles (9.5km)
Height climbed: 1550ft (470m)
Grade: A
Public conveniences: Glenmore
Public transport: Bus service from Aviemore to the ski slopes; stops at Glenmore

A splendid, steep hill climb giving tremendous views in all directions, including towards the Cairngorms. The path is rough, faint and wet in various places.

Turn off the B970 at Coylumbridge and take the ski road up to Glenmore, Heron's Field or lochside car parks where interpretive panels depict the colour coded waymarkers to Shepherd's Hill. This route is one of those listed in the Glenmore Forest Park Guide Map which is available at Glenmore Forest Park Visitor Centre, where further information is available. Adjacent to the Centre is a monument commemorating World War II.

The early part of the route is a gentle climb through mixed woodland. To the left glimpses of a burn can be seen tumbling through the forest. Here and there are small groups of the older, naturally sown Scots pine: relics of the Caledonian pine forest.

Halfway to the summit, at about 1000ft (480m), the path breaks out of the forest, steepens as it heads towards the saddle between Meall a'Bhuachaille and Creagan Gorm *(Blue Hill)* past scattered pine trees.

Once on the saddle the path splits. To the left it climbs to the peak of Creagan Gorm and then continues to Craiggowrie and down to the Sluggan Pass *(3)*. The other path, which this route follows, turns right, up to the summit of the Meall. At the top there is a large cairn which offers some protection from the elements - often necessary - and a chance to admire the splendid view of the Cairngorms and Speyside in relative comfort.

Walk down the path on the opposite side of the hill. This is very steep in places, but the views are superb. The red tin roof of Ryvoan Bothy can be seen at the foot of the hill and beyond that, the loch-studded moorland towards Bynack and Strath Nethy. Turn right at Ryvoan. The path is very clear from this point on.

After ½ mile (0.8km) a path cuts off to the left: this is the Cateran's Road *(the Robber's Road)* to Loch Avon and beyond.

Ryvoan Pass, with its scree-covered slopes between clusters of Scots pine, is a romantic spot. In the days before there were roads, hill passes such as this one were in constant use. Cattle were commonly driven through here: either legally, on their way to southern fairs, or illegally, the booty from some clan raid.

At the heart of the pass is little Lochan Uaine *(Green Loch)*. Oddly enough the waters *are* green, varying from a light turquoise at the water's edge to a deep bottle green.

The path continues beside Allt na Feith Duibhe *(Black Bog Burn)* back into the Caledonian Pinewood Reserve. The track becomes surfaced at Glenmore Lodge (a Scottish Sports Council training centre) and then continues, straight back to the car parks.

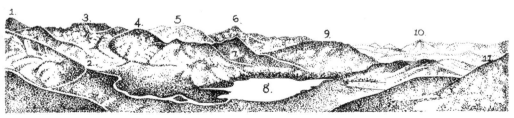

1. *Cairngorm (1245m)* 2. *Coire Cas* 3. *Cairn Lochan (1215m)* 4. *Creag na Leacainn (1053m)* 5. *Braeriach (1296m)* 6. *Sgorran Dubh Mor (1111m)* 7. *Carn Eilrig (742m)* 8. *Loch Morlich* 9. *Creagan Dhubh (848m)* 10. *Creag Dhubh (717m)* 11. *Monadhliath Mountains*

6 Cairngorm

Length: 4 miles (6.5km)
Height climbed: 2000ft (600m)
Grade: A
Public conveniences: Ski centres
Public transport: Bus service between Aviemore and the ski slopes

A steep hill climb above the ski slopes of Cairngorm. The ground is rough, and it can be cold and misty on the top. Superb views.

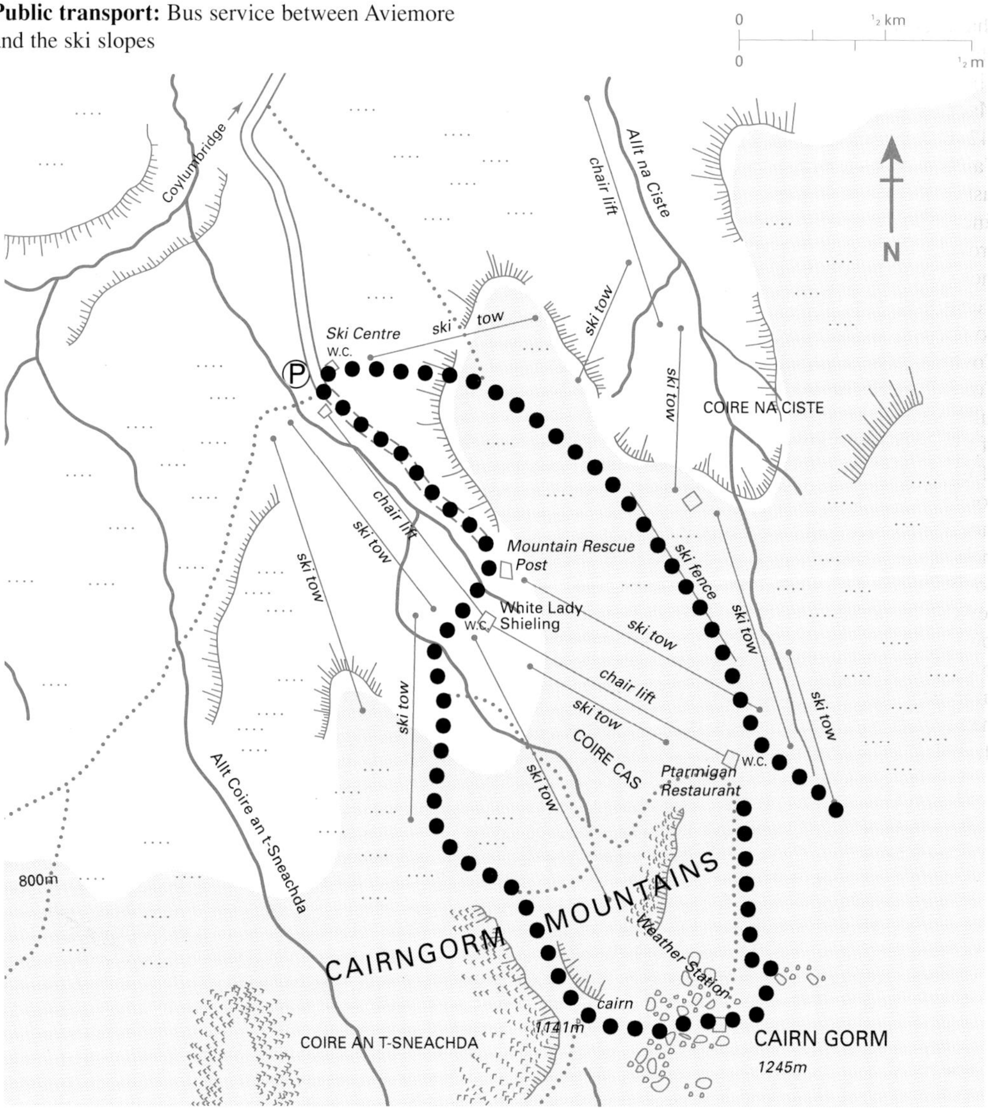

Map labels:

0   ½ km
0   ½ m

N

Coylumbridge

Allt na Ciste
chair lift
ski tow
ski tow

COIRE NA CISTE

Ski Centre
W.C.
ski tow

chair lift
ski tow

ski tow
Mountain Rescue Post
White Lady Shieling
W.C.

ski fence
ski tow
ski tow

chair lift
ski tow
COIRE CAS
Ptarmigan Restaurant
W.C.
ski tow

Allt Coire an t-Sneachda

800m

CAIRNGORM MOUNTAINS

Weather Station

cairn
1141m

COIRE AN T-SNEACHDA

CAIRN GORM
1245m

The highest peak in Scotland is Ben Nevis in Lochaber (4406ft/1342m), but the highest massif is the granite block of the Cairngorms — characterised by their rounded peaks and high plateaux intersected by deep glacial valleys. These hills include four peaks over 4000ft — Ben Macdui (4206ft/1309m), Braeriach (4248ft/1296m), Cairn Toul (4241ft/1291m) and Cairngorm (The Blue Hill) (4084ft/1245m). This last is the most easily accessible of the peaks, since a road was built up to its lower slopes to provide access to the ski slopes — indeed, for those who feel disinclined to climb the hill there is a chairlift to within 600ft (180m) of the summit. To reach the walk take the road from Aviemore to Coylumbridge and then follow the ski road up to Coire Cas. There is a large car park here, and a full range of facilities in the ski centre at the foot of the chair lift. The ski slopes run down the sides of the corrie; where the glaciers of the ice age gouged a concave hollow from the side of the mountain. There is no particular path up the mountain. Start walking up the path along the floor of the corrie, and then cut up to the left, beyond the bottom ski centre. Keeping the ski tow to your left, pick your way across the slope up to the protective ski fences above Coire na Ciste, on to the ridge up to the Ptarmigan Restaurant — the highest in the country — at the top of the chairlift. The going is steep but easy.

The hill has a covering of pink granite chips. It was the colour of this rock which gave the mountains their original Gaelic name: Monadh Ruaidh (The Red Mountains). There is only sparse vegetation. Beyond the restaurant there is a flight of steps to the summit. The surrounding landscape is one of broad, rocky, level ridges and deep corries; the views beyond are too vast and too spectacular to illustrate or describe — just be certain to choose a clear day for the climb; check the forecast and watch for low clouds which can cut visibility completely. Take a detailed map to identify distant landmarks and aid navigation on the way down. Walk westwards to the rocky cairn above Coire Cas and then continue down the ridge of Fiacaill a'Choire Chais to the White Lady Shieling. On this section be careful not to go too close to the corrie edge: there are steep cliffs here. Also, as the snow often lingers late into the summer on these hills, it is important not to venture on to any remaining patches — particularly near the corrie edges. The snow is unstable and often overhangs the cliffs. Among the bird life of the tops, the ptarmigan — white in winter; mottled grey in summer — is the commonest species, but the rarer dotterel and snow bunting may also be seen. One peculiar feature of the area is its herd of reindeer. These animals disappeared from the Highlands about 1000 years ago, but were reintroduced from Lapland in the 1950s.

7 Serpent's Loch

Length: 4 miles (6.5km)
Height climbed: Negligible
Grade: B
Public conveniences: Glenmore
Public transport: Bus service between Aviemore
and the ski slopes; stops at Glenmore

*A level forest walk through a variety of
conifer types and ages, passing Loch
Morlich. Paths good.*

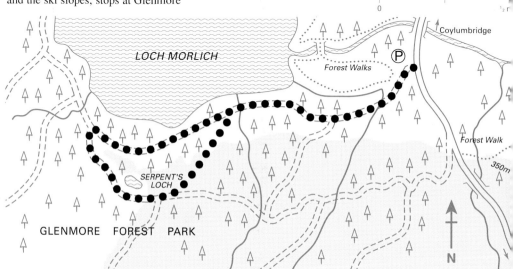

Follow the ski road from Coylumbridge to Loch
Morlich. The car park is just beyond the loch on
the right hand side beyond the river.

A fairly easy walk starting from Heron's Field
car park. The trail is long enough to require good
footwear but does not leave the shelter of the
forest. From the car park follow the forest road
around the southern shore of Loch Morlich. After
1½ miles the road strikes inland from the Loch
and after another ¼ mile reaches Lochan nan
Nathrach - the Serpent's Loch. There are many
splendid views along the way and some time spent
by the peaceful location can be reward enough for
this walk. The return path follows an old railway

line route, used to extract timber during the 1st
World War.

On the outward stretch of the walk the
Cairngorms are visible to the left of the path, the
conical peak of Carn Eilrig being prominent. On
the return route the summit of Meall
a'Bhuachaille *(The Shepherd's Hill) (5),* the most
easterly of the Kincardine Hills, is visible above
the trees, with Creag nan Gall *(The Stranger's
Hill)* across the Ryvoan Pass to its right.

The Serpent's Loch is a tiny lochan surrounded
by trees, near the turn of the walk.

8 Loch an Eilein

Length: 3 miles (5km)
Height climbed: None
Grade: C
Public conveniences: At route
Public transport: None

A short walk on good tracks through an area of great beauty. The loch includes an island with a ruined castle, and is surrounded by a forest of Scots pine.

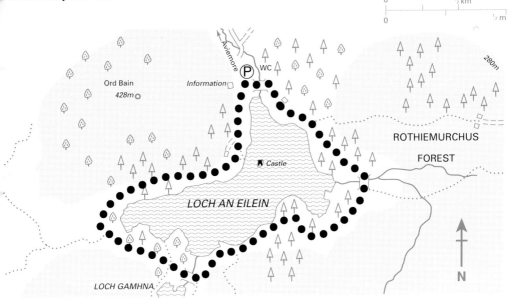

Loch an Eilein translates as 'Loch of the Island', and on the island are the ruins of a castle. The building is linked with the 14th century 'Wolf of Badenoch' — Alexander Stewart: son of King Robert II — whose destructive and unpopular viceroyalty of the Highlands necessitated the use of such impregnable strongholds. There was originally a narrow causeway to the shore, but this was submerged when the loch was dammed to store water for floating logs down to the sawmills. To reach Loch an Eilein turn off the Aviemore to Coylumbridge road about 1 mile (1.5km) from its junction with the B9152 and follow the signs. There is a car park (with a charge), set in a pleasant bowl, surrounded by birch and Scots pine. The path is quite clear. Leaflets about the

route are available at the car park and at a small information pavilion a short way along the route. The path itself is part of the bewildering maze of interconnected tracks through Rothiemurchus and Glenmore *(5,7,3)*, and paths join the main route at various points, leading off to other parts of the forest. One diversion, at the south end of Loch an Eilein, leads round little Loch Gamhna *(Loch of the Stirks)*. The main route generally stays close to the loch, passing through a forest of Scots pine. The castle was a nesting site for ospreys until the species was hunted out of Scotland at the start of the century. It is not unlikely that one of these birds — which have recently begun nesting again in this area — will be seen fishing in the loch.

9 Lower Glen Feshie

Length: 5 miles (8km)
Height climbed: 200ft (50m)
Grade: B
Public conveniences: None
Public transport: None

A walk through a variety of woodlands in and around Glen Feshie. The path is excellent, but there are occasional damp patches.

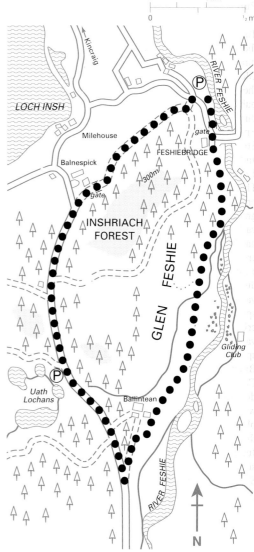

The U-shaped valley of Glen Feshie, which divides the granite mass of the Cairngorms from the lower hills of Badenoch to the east, is a typical Highland valley, formed by the erosion of the glaciers during the last ice age. The area is full of evidence of the departed ice. To reach the start of this walk turn off the B9152 at Kincraig and turn left at the next junction. The Forest Enterprise Car Park and Picnic Site is about 1/2 mile (0.8km) further on, to the left of the road. A path climbs along the edge of the River Feshie and then crosses the road, just before Feshiebridge. Follow the sign to Glen Feshie and Glen Tilt. At first the path runs beside the river, which passes through a narrow rocky defile, but it soon leaves the river and passes through a forest of conifers. After leaving the plantation it drops to the flood plain of the valley, scattered with birch trees, with a long wooded ridge of glacial deposits to the right. The way splits at one point, with the right hand path skirting round the end of the mound. Keep to the left here and cross the small burn. The path now runs close to the river, wide and shallow, meandering through the gravel deposits of the flat valley floor. At the stables at Ballintean Farm keep to the left of the buildings and skirt up the edge of the grounds on to a path in front of a pine plantation. Follow this path on to the metalled road and turn right. Stay with this road till Balnespick; turn right here, behind the farm, and follow the path back to the road, turning right on return to the car park. On this last stretch there are fine views of Loch Insh and the rest of the Spey Valley.

10 Upper Glen Feshie

Length: 8 miles (13km)
Height climbed: 200ft (60m)
Grade: A
Public conveniences: None
Public transport: None

A long walk through a variety of woodland and open moorland in a typical U-shaped Highland glen. Paths rough and wet in places.

To reach upper Glen Feshie take the road across the River Spey at Kincraig. Turn right at the junction and then left on the road signposted to Glen Feshie. About 3 miles (5km) along this road there is a space to park, just before the end of the public road. Walk on along a metalled road through Scots pine — woodland owned by Forest Enterprise. The plantation ends at the cottage of Stronetoper. Please pay attention to the sign here and stay off the surrounding hills between August 1 and October 20 when the stag cull is in progress. The path is quite clear now, 2 miles (3km) to the bridge at Carnachuin. Along this stretch the gradual erosion of the glacial deposits on the valley floor is clearly visible — in places the soil has been swept away by the river, revealing a deep cross-section of fine sands. At Carnachuin there is a monument to the men who trained in the glen during the last war. It is a beautiful spot. The valley widens above the bridge and the river spreads across it in a skein of rocky channels, criss-crossing between the scattered pine on the valley floor. On the far side of the bridge the path splits in three: the right hand fork heading for Braemar and the central path climbing in to the Cairngorms. Follow the left hand fork, returning down the glen. The path becomes damp now as it winds through a conifer plantation. Beyond the plantation is Allt Garbhlach, flowing down from the impressive Coire Garbhlach (*Rugged Corrie*). Jump across at a suitable spot. Cross the next stretch of moorland to reach the bridge above Stronetoper and then follow the path back to the parking place.

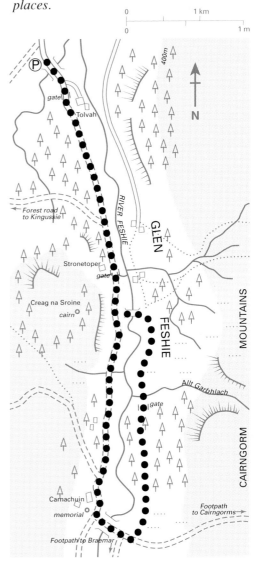

11 Ruthven Barracks

Length: 2 miles (3km) there and back
Height climbed: None
Grade: C
Public conveniences: Kingussie
Public transport: Bus and train services to
Kingussie from north and south

A short walk on metalled roads to the dramatic ruins of Ruthven Barracks. A possible moorland extension on rough pathways.

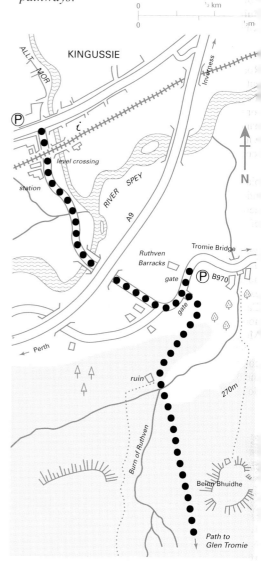

The existing building of Ruthven Barracks was built in 1719 by the Hanoverian troops to help control the area after the 1715 Jacobite rising, but this splendid site had been in use for many years before that. The first castle was built by the Comyns in the 13th Century, and a later building was used by the infamous 'Wolf of Badenoch'.

Start the walk at Kingussie, walking down Ruthven Road towards the station. Carry straight on, across the level crossing. Turn left at the junction.

The ruins sit on a grassy mound, well above the flood plain of the River Spey — which often does flood along this stretch of the river. The roof has been missing since the building was captured and burned by the Jacobite army in 1746, but the high walls of the two main residential blocks and the nearby stables are still largely intact. Return by the same route.

There is a possible extension of this route — for those wearing stout footwear — across the moors to Glen Tromie. Fifty yards (metres) back along the road turn left, through a gate. The path turns sharp right, by a dyke, and then climbs on up the hill, past a ruined cottage, over the Ruthven Burn and on across the moorland. Keep the peak of Beinn Bhuidhe *(Yellow Hill)* to the left. At the top of the hill there is a gate: turn right immediately after this and carry on, eventually bearing left between two hills and dropping down into the steep-sided Glen Tromie.

It is 4 miles (6.5km) from Ruthven to Glen Tromie. Either return by the same route or take the road down the glen, turning left at Tromie Bridge to return to Ruthven. This makes a round trip of 12 miles (19km) from Kingussie.

12 Creag Beg

Length: 3 miles (5km)
Height climbed: 800ft (246m)
Grade: B
Public conveniences: Kingussie
Public transport: Bus and train services to Kingussie from north and south

A brisk hill climb on rough paths. The path is occasionally steep; occasionally invisible. Tremendous views.

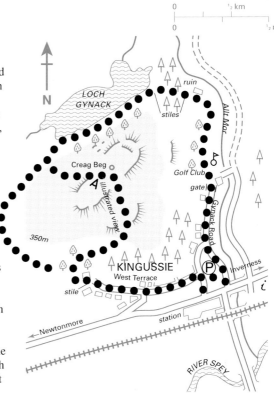

From the centre of Kingussie walk up Gynack Road, to the golf club. Walk in the main gate and cut left, up the side of the first fairway. While on the course keep an eye open for people playing, for their sakes and yours. Cut left through a thin band of woodland and skirt around the 5th green, with its ruined cottage, towards a stile across the fence.

The path is quite clear now, through a conifer plantation, across another fence and along the side of Loch Gynack. The way is rather wet here, through the scrub woodland at the base of Creag Beg.

Once out of the wood the path rises and becomes drier. Wait until the slope to the left is sufficiently shallow and start climbing: there is no particular path. The views from the top are excellent in all directions — east to the Cairngorms and Strathspey; west to Creag Dhubh above Newtonmore, Glen Banchor and the Monadhliath Mountains.

Scramble down the front of the hill, leaving the conifer plantation to the left, and wander through the birch and juniper back to Kingussie. Turn left down West Terrace to reach the town centre.

1. *Carn Dearg Mor (858m)* 2. *Cruaidhleac (640m)* 3. *Kingussie* 4. *Mullach Bheag* 5. *River Spey*
6. *Creag Bheag (491m)* 7. *Garbh Mheall Mor* 8. *Meall na Cuaich (951m)* 9. *Geal Charn (916m)*
10. *Cruba-Beag* 11. *Meall Liath (911m)* 12. *Newtonmore*

13 Green Bothy

Length: 6 miles (9.5km) there and back
Height climbed: 750ft (220m)
Grade: B
Public conveniences: Newtonmore
Public transport: Bus and train services to
Newtonmore from north and south

*A most enjoyable moorland walk, giving
fine views of the Monadhliaths and the
Hills of Badenoch. The path is very wet in
places.*

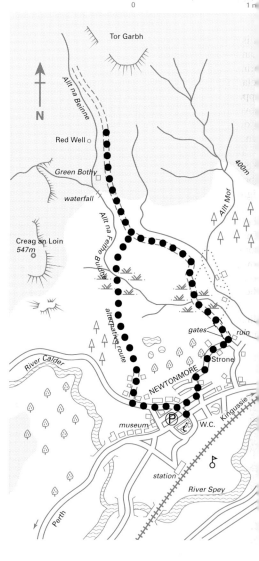

The town of Newtonmore was originally built as a
clearance village for the people who were evicted
from the surrounding hills.

This route starts in the main car park off the
High Street, behind the Gables Inn. Turn right in
front of the Church of Scotland, past a pottery and
the unique Aqua-theatre. After 300 yards turn left
up a hill and, keeping the phone box on your left,
cross a cattle grid taking you out on to the moor
above the village. Half a mile further on, just past
a passing place sign, turn left by a dilapidated
barn taking you out on to the moor. Then follow a
clear path up the hill and through a second gate.
The path splits at one point — keep left, then
cross Allt na Feithe Buidhe *(The Burn of the
Yellow Bog)* by a small bridge.

As the path crosses the moor, the hills close in
around a small glen. At the head of the glen is the
site of an old hut, perched beside a waterfall.

Continue up the hill beyond the bothy for a few
minutes. There is a small cairn to the left of the
path, and a stone with the initials JD. By the burn
to the left of the path at this point there is a spring.
The soil around it has been dyed red by the iron in
the water.

Either return by the same route or turn right at
the bottom of the glen and follow the alternative
route shown on the map. This path can be very
wet. The track is indistinct until it reaches a fence
corner. Follow the fence line to the right towards
a gate 200 yards across the burn. The path crosses
several boggy areas but is clear enough if you
head for the corner of the conifer plantation.
Keeping the wood to your right, follow the old
peat road through a meadow to the public road
which takes you back to Newtonmore.

14 Dun da Lamh

Length: 4 miles (6.5km)
Height climbed: 600ft (190m)
Grade: B
Public conveniences: None
Public transport: None

A forest walk to an old hill fort, with fine views of upper Speyside and Strath Mashie. Path good, but rough near the top.

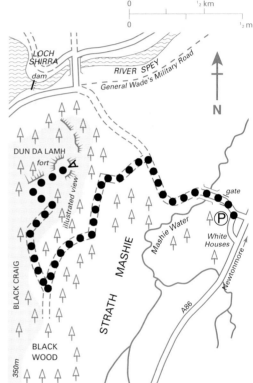

It is difficult to say how old the fort at Dun da Lamh *(Fort of the Two Hands)* is, but such a prime defensive site must surely have been utilised relatively early, and forts of this kind began to appear in Scotland around 500 BC. The tree-covered hill on which it sits rises steeply like the prow of a ship, some 600ft (180m) from the flat land at the confluence of the Spey and the Mashie.

To reach the walk take the A86 from Newtonmore, parking by a row of white houses about 1½ miles (2.5km) beyond Laggan, to the right of the road.

The route is simple. Follow the estate road over the Mashie Water and turn left at the junction. The path runs along the side of the hill through commercial forestry and then turns back, sharply, towards the summit. Where the path ends cut up to the left, along the edge of the plantation, and then approach the fort along the top of the ridge.

The view from the summit extends in every direction, including the Monadhliaths, Strathspey and the Hills of Badenoch (see below).

Return by the same route.

1. *The Monadhliath Mountains* **2.** *Marg na Craige* **3.** *Creag Dhubh (717m)* **4.** *Laggan* **5.** *Strathmashie*
6. *Strathspey*

15 Pattack Forest

Length: 2¹/₂ miles (4km) there and back
Height climbed: 500ft (150m)
Grade: C
Public conveniences: None
Public transport: None

A short steep walk through commercial forestry to a viewpoint above Strath Mashie.

To reach this walk take the A86 road from Newtonmore to Laggan. About 3 ¹/₂ miles (5.5km) beyond Laggan there is a car park to the right of the road.

On the opposite side of the road are the lower Falls of Pattack, and a short detour will provide a good view of the lowest basin. It is a romantic spot, with the water thundering into a wide, rocky pool, overhung by rowans, birch, pine and larch. This point is the watershed of Scotland: all rivers to the east of here empty into the North Sea, but the Pattack flows to the Atlantic.

Recross the road to the car park. The route is perfectly clear, wandering up the hillside through dense forestry, to the viewpoint at Black Craig. The view is extensive. West — back down the path — is Loch Laggan, which provides water for the aluminium smelter at Fort William. On a clear day Ben Nevis can be seen beyond the loch. Below is Strath Mashie while, looking down the Spey, there is a good view of the peak of Creag Dhubh above Newtonmore.

A similar but rather better view can be had from Dun da Lamh *(14)*, but the walk is longer and the climb higher.

Return by the same route.

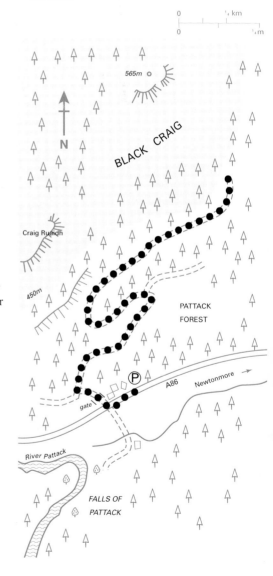